I Live in Laurel

A Children's History of Laurel, Mississippi

by Karen C. Rasberry
& Cyndi Trest

Illustrated by Adam Trest

Designed by Erin Rasberry Napier

LOBLOLLY
press

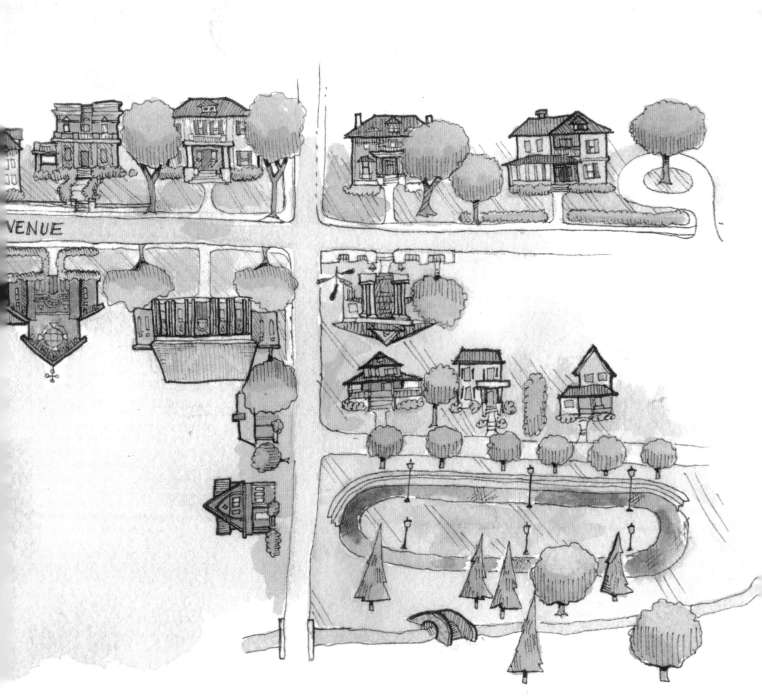

VENUE

I Live in Laurel
Copyright © 2013 by Loblolly Press

402 North Magnolia Street
Suite B
Laurel, Mississippi 39440

Authored by Karen C. Rasberry & Cyndi Trest
Illustrated by Adam Trest
Designed and edited by Erin Rasberry Napier

ISBN-13: 978-1492955597
ISBN-10: 1492955590

Published October 2013
First Edition

For Cyndi
& the children of Laurel—
past, present, and future

My name is Anne.
I live in a small and beautiful city named Laurel, Mississippi. Laurel became a city a long time ago in 1882.

Before people moved here,
straight, tall pine trees grew
where houses and stores are
now. Deer, rabbits, squirrels,
coyotes, and other wild animals
roamed freely.

I like living in Laurel because I can look out my front window and see a pretty park and a big, white bank. I can see almost the entire downtown from my house.
Well, I don't really live in a house.
My mom and dad call it a loft,
but I pretend it's a
tree house.

I can look out my back window and see city hall, the courthouse and lots of busy people going to and fro.

I like Laurel because there is always something fun to do.

In the spring there's Day in the Park where I can eat corndogs, have my face painted, and listen to music while I stretch out on a blanket with my family.

In the summertime

we go to the farmer's market where I get homemade cookies and my mother buys fresh vegetables and fruit. Sometimes we take lawn chairs and watch a movie in the park beside the Laurel Little Theatre.

In the fall

I can go to the pumpkin patch with my friends to pick out the biggest pumpkin for Halloween, and there's the Loblolly Festival where people come from miles around to celebrate the founding of our town. There's a lumberjack named Big Ben, and woodcarvers, and booths filled with all kinds of things to buy.

In the winter we always go to the Christmas tree lighting in Pinehurst Park. It is so exciting to see the lights and hear the carol singers with my friends and family.

Everyone in the whole town waits in line to eat hot, buttery pancakes before the Christmas parade starts. The parade is very long and filled with floats, bands, horses and motorcycles.

I love living in Laurel every season of the year. Don't you?

I like Laurel most of all because I can put on my pink tutu, run downstairs, and with four skips and a hop, arrive in front of the coffee shop. I don't drink coffee, but I love the way it smells in there. The best thing about the coffee shop is that my friend Mr. George is always there working and writing. Mr. George is a famous writer who grew up in Laurel, traveled the world, then came back home because it's a happy place for creative people to live.

I don't know how old Mr. George is, but I bet he lived here in 1882 because he knows everything about Laurel. I like Mr. George because he wears shorts in the winter and a straw hat in the summer to protect his face from the sun.

He reminds me of Santa Claus, but he isn't fat at all. Because he didn't own a car when he lived in New York City, he still walks everywhere he goes.

He always carries chocolates in his pockets and he doesn't mind sharing them.

Laurel is a nice place to live because in five skips and two hops from my house I can be in the courtyard of the Laurel Little Theatre.

ANNIE
AUDITIONS
TUES. NIGHT

A long time ago, it was a fancy movie house called the Arabian Theatre.

Now, it's where adults and children like me get to perform in plays and musicals in front of hundreds of people. Being up on that stage is the most fun! I've decided to become an actress, or a ballerina, or an artist, or a mermaid when I grow up.

What do you want to be when you grow up?

One day my mother and I were leaving the Laurel Little Theatre and bumped right into Mr. George as he was walking home.

He asked if we would like to join him on his walk up Fifth Avenue. It was a pretty day, so we did just that.

Mr. George was happy to have someone to talk to along the way.

He told us that Laurel began
in the 1800s as a timber town.

The town needed a name, but it was such a dirty, rough place that nobody wanted the town named after them. They decided to name the little town

Laurel

after the laurel bushes that grew all around.

Laurel soon became a boomtown because of the sawmills. The lumber had to be taken to other cities to be shipped all over the world. Timber was to Laurel what gold was to California. People came here from all over the country to work in the sawmills and to make money. They built cabins near the mills. Churches, stores, a hotel, and boarding house soon sprang up.

For a time in Laurel's history the town was known as the "yellow pine capitol of the world" because more pine lumber was shipped from here than anywhere else in the world.

In 1891, George and Silas Gardiner, and their brother-in-law, Lauren Eastman, bought an old sawmill and thousands of acres of land. The beautiful homes and churches they built are still standing today. Mr. George said that almost all of the lumber mills closed in the 1930s,

but Laurel kept growing thanks to all the other big companies that started here.

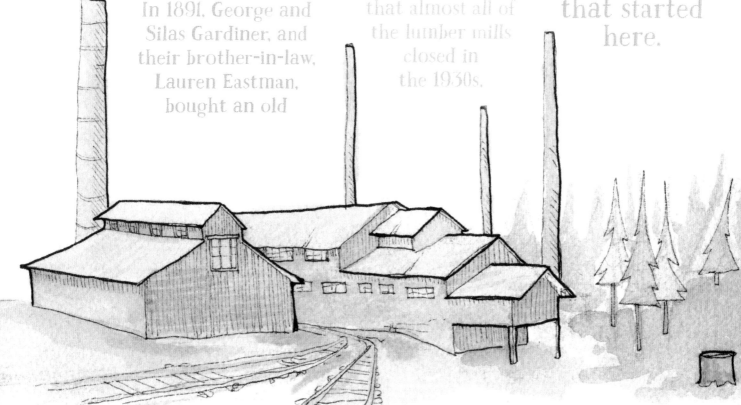

Mr. George, my mother, my little brother, and I strolled past the beautiful old churches along Fifth Avenue. We stopped for a moment in front of St. John's Day School.

George Gardiner built it as his home when Laurel was in the timber boom.

A few steps past the school stands **White Oak**, built by Phil Gardiner. It was once the rectory for the Episcopal church. My mother says that "rectory" is a fancy word for a priest's house.

We stopped at the corner under huge oak trees as **Mr. George told us the story of Lauren Rogers.**

Lauren Rogers was young and newly married. He was the son of one of Laurel's founding fathers. He became sick when he was still a young man, and after he passed away his family built a beautiful museum in his memory.

The Lauren Rogers Museum of Art opened in 1923. It was Mississippi's first art museum! Catherine Marshall Gardiner, George Gardiner's wife, gave many of her collections to the museum, including her basket collection.

It is known all over the world for its fine collection of artwork. Each year, thousands of people come to see it.

The second smallest basket in the world is my very favorite thing to see at the museum.

As we crossed the street to the next corner, Mr. George began to tell us about some of the people from Laurel who have done amazing things. He pointed to a lovely white house with large round columns. It was built by John Lindsey, the inventor of the Lindsey wagon.

He invented a large, eight-wheeled wagon that could pull logs out of the woods and swamps. Lindsey Wagons were used all over the world before the bulldozer was invented and in both World War I and World War II they were used to haul heavy loads for the soldiers.

William H. Mason was an inventor who worked with Thomas Edison, the inventor of the light bulb. He thought of a way to use the wood chips left over from the sawmills to make a new kind of wood that could be used on houses, and he called it Masonite. Masonite is used all over the world.

Do you go to Mason Park or Mason Elementary School? These places are named after William H. Mason.

We walked a little further to the home of Alexander and Elizabeth Chisholm where Leontyne Price's aunt once worked. They used their wealth to help others succeed.

With their help, Leontyne Price became a world-famous opera singer at the Metropolitan Opera in New York City!

She played Aida, a Nubian princess, and she went on to sing all over the world. She grew up in Laurel, just like me.

Not only is Laurel home of inventors and singers, it is also the hometown of great athletes, leaders, and actors.

Ralph Boston won a gold medal in the 1960 Olympics.

He set a world record with his 27 foot broad jump.

He went on to win a silver medal in 1964 and a bronze medal in 1968.

I think I will try to win an Olympic medal, or learn to sing opera, or invent something useful one day.

We kept walking to Gardiner Park to learn some more about Laurel.

Have you ever heard of Central Park in New York City?

It was designed by the famous landscape architect Frederick Law Olmstead.

Guess what?

In 1909, George Gardiner hired his company to design Gardiner Park. Our park has big, shady trees, and a track where people can walk. There is a field for playing sports and a jungle gym to climb!

Mr. George said he graduated from George S. Gardiner High School a long time ago.

That beautiful building is still there at the north end of Gardiner Park. He says that Laurel has always had wonderful teachers. L.T. Ellis, Nora Davis, and R.H. Watkins were some of the first teachers who believed that the children of Laurel deserved the best education possible.

L.T. Ellis

started the Oak Park Vocational School that taught agriculture and trade. He spent his whole life teaching children.

Nora Davis

began teaching in 1906 in a one-room log building. She became a principal and now some of my friends go to an elementary school named after her.

R.H. Watkins

was in charge of the schools in Laurel for 40 years. Laurel's public high school is named after him.

My mother is a teacher!
Maybe I will become one too, instead of a mermaid.

Walking and talking with Mr. George was like talking with a history book. It seems impossible to think how much the world has changed since 1882 when Laurel was brand new. He remembers all the old businesses downtown, where they were located and who worked in them. He remembers the old days like it was yesterday, but he also likes the way Laurel is today with its shops and friendly people.

I like the way it is now, living in a loft with my parents and baby brother. **Living here makes me think I can become anything my heart desires.** I may become a writer, or a ballerina, or a singer, or an inventor, or an Olympian, or even a mermaid in a pink tutu.

My name is Anne.
I live in Laurel,
Mississippi.

AFTERWORD

Cyndi Trest was a beloved local teacher who positively impacted the lives of many children. She always dreamed of writing a children's book. Before she passed away, she compiled a children's history of Laurel. Award-winning writer Karen C. Rasberry used that history to create the story of a little girl who loves living in Laurel. Adam Trest, Cyndi's son, is a gifted illustrator who lives in Laurel. The book designer, Erin Rasberry Napier, owns and operates Lucky Luxe Couture Correspondence from her studio in downtown Laurel. Anne is the daughter of Dawn and Michael Trest, as well as Cyndi's granddaughter. The character Mr. George (McNeill) is a popular columnist and a friend to many in downtown Laurel. This collaboration evolved out of our love for Laurel and to help fill the void that Cyndi's passing left for so many people. We think that she is very happy to know that her dream did come true.

Made in the USA
San Bernardino, CA
26 July 2014